Python for the Busy Java Developer

The Language, Syntax, and Ecosystem

Deepak Sarda

Apress®

Python for the Busy Java Developer

Deepak Sarda
Singapore, Singapore

ISBN-13 (pbk): 978-1-4842-3233-0 ISBN-13 (electronic): 978-1-4842-3234-7
https://doi.org/10.1007/978-1-4842-3234-7

Library of Congress Control Number: 2017960940

Cover image designed by Freepik

Managing Director: Welmoed Spahr
Editorial Director: Todd Green
Acquisitions Editor: Todd Green
Development Editor: James Markham
Technical Reviewer: Chaim Krause
Coordinating Editor: Jill Balzano
Copy Editor: Kim Burton weisman
Compositor: SPi Global
Indexer: SPi Global
Artist: SPi Global

Distributed to the book trade worldwide by Springer Science+Business Media New York, 233 Spring Street, 6th Floor, New York, NY 10013. Phone 1-800-SPRINGER, fax (201) 348-4505, e-mail orders-ny@springer-sbm.com, or visit www.springeronline.com. Apress Media, LLC is a California LLC and the sole member (owner) is Springer Science + Business Media Finance Inc (SSBM Finance Inc). SSBM Finance Inc is a **Delaware** corporation.

For information on translations, please e-mail rights@apress.com, or visit http://www.apress.com/rights-permissions.

Apress titles may be purchased in bulk for academic, corporate, or promotional use. eBook versions and licenses are also available for most titles. For more information, reference our Print and eBook Bulk Sales web page at http://www.apress.com/bulk-sales.

Any source code or other supplementary material referenced by the author in this book is available to readers on GitHub via the book's product page, located at www.apress.com/9781484232330. For more detailed information, please visit http://www.apress.com/source-code.

Printed on acid-free paper

Table of Contents

About the Author v

About the Technical Reviewer vii

Acknowledgments ix

Introduction xi

Chapter 1: The Language 1

What Is Python? 1

History... 3

Installation 5

Tools... 6

Summary.. 12

Chapter 2: The Syntax 13

Hello World... 13

Basic Constructs 14

Basic Types 16

Numbers.. 16

Strings 17

Collections 18

Fun with Lists... 19

Functions 25

Functions and Tuples.. 29

Functions Inside Functions... 31

Classes 34

    Inheritance 37

    Polymorphism 38

    Getting Dynamic! 39

Protocols 42

Organizing Code 45

    Importing code 45

    The main() Method 48

Summary 57

Chapter 3: The Ecosystem **59**

A Rich Ecosystem 59

    Popular Tools 60

    Popular Frameworks 62

Summary 65

Chapter 4: The Zen of Python **67**

Appendix: References **69**

Index **71**

About the Author

Deepak Sarda has been working as a software developer for more than twelve years, in multiple business domains and in a variety of technologies. He has worked on several high-performance, server-side applications written in Java, and has done web development and systems automation work in Python.

He lives in Singapore with his lovely wife and their adorable daughters. He can be found online at `antrix.net` or @antrix on Twitter.

He'd love to hear what you've to say about this book. Please email him at `deepak@antrix.net`.

About the Technical Reviewer

 **Chaim Krause** is an expert computer programmer with over 30 years of experience to prove it. He has worked as a lead tech support engineer for ISPs as early as 1995, as a senior developer support engineer with Borland for Delphi, and has worked in Silicon Valley for over a decade in various roles, including technical support engineer and developer support engineer. He is currently a military simulation specialist for the US Army's Command and General Staff College, working on projects such as developing serious games for use in training exercises.

He has also authored several video training courses on Linux topics and has been a technical reviewer on more than 20 books, including *iOS Code Testing* by Abhishek Mishra (Apress, 2017*), Android Apps for Absolute Beginners* by Wallace Jackson (Apress, 2017), and *C# and XML Primer: XML Essentials for C# and .NET Development* by Jonathan Hartwell (Apress, 2017). It seems only natural that he would be an avid gamer and have his own electronics lab and server room in his basement. He currently resides in Leavenworth, Kansas, with his loving partner, Ivana, and a menagerie of four-legged companions: their two dogs, Dasher and Minnie, and their three cats, Pudems, Talyn, and Alaska.

Acknowledgments

I'd always heard it being said, but only now do I truly realize it: *writing a book is hard work!* It would have been harder still had it not been for the support from my family and friends.

I wish to especially thank Hitesh Sarda, Rohit Sharma, and Srijith Nair for the incredibly detailed and thoughtful feedback that they provided as I wrote this book. I owe many thanks to them.

I must also acknowledge the constant encouragement that I received from my wife, Sonika. I can't thank her enough for her patience and support as I took time out to write this book.

Introduction

Hello There!

If you are reading this book, then chances are that you are a busy Java developer who is interested in learning Python. If so, I hope that by the time you are done reading this short book.

- You will have gained sufficient familiarity with the Python language syntax so that you're able to read some code and understand what it is doing.

- You will have had enough orientation to be able to navigate the Python ecosystem of libraries and tools.

This book is *not* for the beginner programmer. I assume that you are comfortable programming in Java (or a similar language like C#), and hence, I will not bore you with explanations of basic concepts like variables, functions, and classes.

About the Book

This book is divided into three broad chapters:

- The Language

- The Syntax

- The Ecosystem

In the first chapter, we take a brief look at the Python language and learn what it has to offer. Next, we'll get down to the details of the syntax before wrapping up with a look at the wider ecosystem surrounding the Python language.

CHAPTER 1

The Language

Let's start our Python journey by first gaining an understanding of what Python has to offer that's different from Java. I'll then help you get setup with Python before we dive into the language's syntax in the next chapter.

What Is Python?

Python is an "open source, general-purpose programming language that is dynamic, strongly typed, object-oriented, functional, memory-managed, and fun to use." Those are a lot of adjectives for one sentence! Let's unpack them one at a time.

Python is distributed under an **open source**, BSD-style license called the Python Software Foundation License Agreement. It is a very permissive license that allows great flexibility in how Python can be used. Python's development is done in the open by a large and diverse community of volunteers.

Python is **general purpose** in that you can use it to build a variety of applications running the gamut from simple scripts and command-line tools to desktop and web applications, network servers, scientific applications, and more.

We know that Java is a statically typed language; that is, the types are checked and enforced at compile time. In contrast, Python is **dynamic**, which means that the types are checked only at runtime. But Python is

D. Sarda, *Python for the Busy Java Developer*, https://doi.org/10.1007/978-1-4842-3234-7_1

also **strongly typed**, just like Java. You can only execute operations that are supported by the target type.

Another way to think about this is that in Java, both variables and objects have types associated with them; whereas in Python, only objects have types, not the variables that they are bound to. In Java, when we declare

```
MyType obj = new MyType()
```

The obj variable is declared of type MyType and then the newly instantiated object of type MyType is assigned to it. In contrast, in Python, the same declaration would read

```
obj = MyType()
```

Ignoring the missing new keyword (which Python doesn't have), obj is simply a name that is bound to the object on the right, which happens to be of type MyType. We can even reassign obj in the very next line—obj = MyOtherType()—and it wouldn't be a problem. In Java, this reassignment would fail to compile[1] while in Python, the program will run and will only fail at runtime if we try to execute an operation via obj that is incompatible with the type assigned to it at that point in time.

Python is **object oriented** and supports all the standard OOP features that Java has like creation of types using classes, encapsulation of state, inheritance, polymorphism, and so forth. It even goes beyond Java and supports features such as multiple inheritance, operator overloading, meta-programming, and so forth.

Python also supports a rich set of **functional** programming features and idioms. In Python, functions are first-class objects that can be created, manipulated, and passed around just like any other object. While its emphasis on functional programming might not be as focused as say

---

[1] Unless MyOtherType happens to be a subclass of MyType.

2

Clojure, Python certainly offers much more to the functional programmer than Java.[2]

Another similarity between the languages is in terms of manual **memory management**, in that there is none. The language runtime takes care of correctly allocating and freeing up memory, saving the programmer from the drudgery—and mistakes—of manually managing memory. Having said that, the JVM garbage collectors are much, much better performing than the Python GC. This can become a concern depending on the type of application you are building.

Finally, and above all, Python is *fun* and a joy to use. This is a strong claim to make but I hope that by the time you are done reading this book, you'll agree with me and the millions of other Python programmers out there!

History

Python is the brainchild of a Dutch programmer named Guido van Rossum. He started working on it when he got frustrated with the ABC language in the late 1980s and after some years of private development, he released the first version of Python in 1994. This actually makes Python older than Java, the first version of which was released in 1996, a full two years later! A comparison of the two languages is shown in Table 1-1.

---

[2]Even after the introduction of lambdas in Java 8.

3

Table 1-1. *Historical comparison of Java and Python*

Java	Python
James Gosling	Guido van Rossum
From C++/Oak	From ABC
1.0 - Jan 1996	1.0 - Jan 1994
9.0 - Sep 2017	3.6 - Dec 2016
JSR	PEP
Commercial	Community

Note   I'll use this tabular format to compare and contrast Python and Java whenever it makes sense.

Since then, the language has continued to refine and evolve, with Python 2.0 being released in 2000. As of this writing, the 2.x versions are the most widely deployed.

In version 3.0, the language designers decided to break backward compatibility in order to clean up some of the accumulated language warts. Although this has been good from a language perspective, it has been a significant hindrance to those upgrading from 2.x to 3.x. Imagine if Sun had decided to introduce generics in Java 5 *without* type erasure, thus breaking backward compatibility. The Java language would've been much nicer today but the transition period would've been difficult, to say the least. That is the kind of transition the Python user community is going through right now.

Note   Since 2.x is still the most widely used version of Python, this book will cover Python 2.x features and syntax, calling out any differences with 3.x from time to time.

From the outset, Python's development has been done in the open with a community of volunteers contributing to the language and the core libraries. Any language changes are proposed and discussed through a process called PEP (*Python Enhancement Proposals*), with Guido having final say in deciding the outcome. For his stewardship and continuous involvement in the development of Python, Guido is affectionately called the "Benevolent Dictator For Life." He also periodically writes a Python History blog[3] chronicling the evolution of various language features.

Installation

This book is full of example code, and the best way to follow along is to actually try these examples by yourself. To do this, you'll obviously need to install Python on your system. But an easier way is to check if you already have access to a system with Python installed! Almost all systems running Linux should have Python preinstalled. Recent versions of Mac OS X also come with Python preinstalled. Just open a command shell on either of these two systems and type in python. If you get a Python shell prompt, you are all set! The version of Python installed may be a bit outdated but it should be sufficient to get started.

---

[3]http://python-history.blogspot.com/

Tip   As a lightweight alternative, you can try an online Python environment, such as `http://repl.it/`. The examples in this book are all simple enough to work there.

Tools

Python source code is organized in files with a `.py` extension. The `python` executable interprets the source code and translates it into a Python language–specific bytecode that is stored in `.pyc` files. This bytecode is then executed by the Python virtual machine, which is also invoked by the same `python` executable. Although this sounds like two steps, in reality, it is just one step with the bytecode generation happening on the fly.

This is in contrast to Java (see Table 1-2), where the responsibilities for the parsing and compilation of source code and the actual execution of the compiled bytecode are split between `javac` and `java` respectively. In Python, the `python` executable handles both steps. In fact, `.pyc` files are, in effect, just intermediate caches to hold the translated bytecode. They are not strictly necessary for execution. If you deleted the `.pyc` files, they'd simply be regenerated the next time you ran the `.py` files.

Table 1-2. *Comparison of Tools*

Java	Python
.java	.py
.class	.pyc
Java.exe + javac.exe	python.exe
IntelliJ IDEA	PyCharm
Eclipse JDT	PyDev
Java 9 JShell	REPL

There are multiple IDEs available for writing Python code. PyDev, based on the Eclipse framework, and PyCharm, based on the IntelliJ IDEA framework, are two of the more popular choices. While having an IDE is nice, it is perfectly feasible to write Python code using a plain text editor such as Vim[4] or Sublime Text.

One interesting feature of Python that's missing in Java is the REPL, short for *Read Eval Print Loop*. A quick demo would be useful here. If you've got access to a Python installation (follow the instructions in the "Installation" section of this chapter), go ahead and launch a python shell, as follows:

```
antrix@dungeon:~$ python
Python 2.7.5+ (default, Feb 27 2014, 19:39:55)
[GCC 4.8.1] on linux2
Type "help", "copyright", "credits" or "license" for more
information.
>>>
```

When you run the python executable in this manner, it starts up in an *interactive* mode. The first few lines contain information such as the version and the underlying operating system. After that, you are presented with the >>> prompt. This is where all your interaction with Python will occur. The python shell is running a *loop*, which will *read* everything that you type in at this prompt, *evaluate* what it has read, and then *print* the result. Thus the name, REPL.

Let's try it out:

```
>>> 10 + 10
20
>>>
```

---

[4]Yes, Emacs is fine too.

We typed in 10 + 10 at the prompt and hit the Enter key. The Python REPL read this value, evaluated it, and printed the result. Then it went back to the prompt to wait for our next input. Let's try the following variable assignment:

```
>>> x = 10
>>>
```

In this case, we didn't see any output because what we entered was just a statement, not an expression. But it did modify the state of the python shell. If we query for x again, we'll find this:

```
>>> x = 10
>>> x
10
>>>
```

Let's call one of the built-in functions named help.

```
>>> help(x)

Help on int object:
class int(object)
 |  int(x=0) -> int or long
 |  int(x, base=10) -> int or long
 |
 |  Convert a number or string to an integer, or return 0 if no
    arguments are given
:q

>>>
```

Calling help on any object brings up a paged view of what is, effectively, the Javadoc for the object's class. To exit the help view, just type q at the : prompt and you'll be back at the >>> prompt.

The full documentation view for an object can be quite verbose. If you just want a quick overview of what attributes an object supports, use the dir function.

```
>>> dir(x)

['__abs__', '__add__', '__and__', '__class__', '__cmp__', '__
coerce__', '__delattr__', '__div__', '__divmod__', '__doc__',
'__float__', '__floordiv__', '__format__', '__getattribute__',
'__getnewargs__', '__hash__', '__hex__', '__index__', '__
init__', '__int__', '__invert__', '__long__', '__lshift__',
'__mod__', '__mul__', '__neg__', '__new__', '__nonzero__', '__
oct__', '__or__', '__pos__', '__pow__', '__radd__', '__rand__',
'__rdiv__', '__rdivmod__', '__reduce__', '__reduce_ex__', '__
repr__', '__rfloordiv__', '__rlshift__', '__rmod__', '__rmul__',
'__ror__', '__rpow__', '__rrshift__', '__rshift__', '__rsub__',
'__rtruediv__', '__rxor__', '__setattr__', '__sizeof__',
'__str__', '__sub__', '__subclasshook__', '__truediv__', '__
trunc__', '__xor__', 'bit_length', 'conjugate', 'denominator',
'imag', 'numerator', 'real']

>>>
```

Ignoring the funky double-underscores for now, what dir(x) returned is effectively a *directory* of all the attributes available on the object. You can access any of them using the . (dot) syntax.

```
>>> x.numerator
10
>>> x.denominator
1
>>> x.conjugate
<built-in method conjugate of int object at 0x9e9a274>
```

```
>>> x.conjugate()
10
```

You can also use the dir() function without any argument to get a list of *built-ins*.

```
>>> dir()

['__builtins__', '__doc__', '__name__', '__package__']

>>> dir(__builtins__)

['ArithmeticError', 'AssertionError', 'AttributeError',
'BaseException', 'BufferError', 'BytesWarning',
'DeprecationWarning', 'EOFError', 'Ellipsis',
'EnvironmentError', 'Exception', 'False', 'FloatingPointError',
'FutureWarning', 'GeneratorExit', 'IOError', 'ImportError',
'ImportWarning', 'IndentationError', 'IndexError', 'KeyError',
'KeyboardInterrupt', 'LookupError', 'MemoryError',
'NameError', 'None', 'NotImplemented', 'NotImplementedError',
'OSError', 'OverflowError', 'PendingDeprecationWarning',
'ReferenceError'ror', 'RuntimeError', 'RuntimeWarning',
'StandardError', 'StopIteration', 'SyntaxError',
'SyntaxWarning', 'SystemError', 'SystemExit', 'TabError',
'True', 'TypeError', 'UnboundLocalError', 'UnicodeDecodeError',
'UnicodeEncodeError', 'UnicodeError', 'UnicodeTranslateError',
'UnicodeWarning', 'UserWarning', 'ValueError', 'Warning',
'ZeroDivisionError', '_', '__debug__', '__doc__', '__import__',
'__name__', '__package__', 'abs', 'all', 'any', 'apply',
'basestring', 'bin', 'bool', 'buffer', 'bytearray', 'bytes',
'callable', 'chr', 'classmethod', 'cmp', 'coerce', 'compile',
'complex', 'copyright', 'credits', 'delattr', 'dict', 'dir',
'divmod', 'enumerate', 'eval', 'execfile', 'exit', 'file',
```

```
'filter', 'float', 'format', 'frozenset', 'getattr', 'globals',
'hasattr', 'hash', 'help', 'hex', 'id', 'input', 'int',
'intern', 'isinstance', 'issubclass', 'iter', 'len', 'license',
'list', 'locals', 'long', 'map', 'max', 'memoryview', 'min',
'next', 'object', 'oct', 'open', 'ord', 'pow', 'print',
'property', 'quit', 'range', 'raw_input', 'reduce', 'reload',
'repr', 'reversed', 'round', 'set', 'setattr', 'slice',
'sorted', 'staticmethod', 'str', 'sum', 'super', 'tuple',
'type', 'unichr', 'unicode', 'vars', 'xrange', 'zip']

>>>
```

This gives a list of functions and other objects that are *built-in* and do not have to be imported from other packages. This is analogous to how everything defined in the java.lang package is available everywhere in Java without having to explicitly import it.

Tip   The dir and help functions are extremely useful when doing exploratory development in a Python interactive shell.

There's one last thing I wish to show before we wrap up this section. Let's create a new file named hello.py with the following contents:

```
print "Hello There!"
x = 10 + 10
print "The value of x is", x
```

Now execute python, passing in this file as an argument:

```
antrix@dungeon:~$ python hello.py
Hello There!
The value of x is 20
antrix@dungeon:~$
```

This is more along the lines of a traditional development process: write code in a file and then execute that file. This also demonstrates how the python executable combines the role of `javac` and `java` in one process.

With that brief demo of Python, we are ready to explore the language's syntax.

Summary

In this chapter, we learned that Python is not just a *scripting* language but a general-purpose programming language with a long history behind it. We then got familiar with the python executable, the Python counterpart of the java and javac executables.

We also looked at the Python REPL environment, which is a great way to interactively try out Python. If you still don't have the REPL set up, I urge you to do so now because the next chapter makes extensive use of it as we dive into the nitty-gritty details of the language's syntax!

CHAPTER 2

The Syntax

This chapter is the heart of the book. It is a deep dive into Python language features. I explain them using short code fragments that you can easily try out yourself.

We start by introducing the basic data types and built-in collections such as *dictionaries* and *sets*, with a special emphasis on *lists*. We'll then dive into *functions* and discover their power as a first-class language feature.

Moving on to *classes*, we'll find out how flexible Python is as an object-oriented language, especially compared to Java. We'll then explore *protocols*, which extend the language's syntax to your own types.

Finally, we'll discuss the concepts of *modules* and *packages* as a means of organizing Python code.

As you can see, it is going to be a long chapter. So grab some coffee and let's get started!

Hello World

```
>>> print "Hello World"
Hello World
>>>
```

Well, that was easy! Moving on ...

© Deepak Sarda 2017
D. Sarda, *Python for the Busy Java Developer*, https://doi.org/10.1007/978-1-4842-3234-7_2

Tip   In Python 3, the `print` keyword has been replaced with the `print()` function.

Basic Constructs

Here's a bit of Python code that, well, I don't have to tell you what it does, do I? Most Python code is like this: eminently readable and almost pseudo-code-like.

```
>>> numbers = [1, 2, 3, 4, 5, 6, 7, 8, 9]                    ①
>>> odd_numbers = []                                         ②
>>>
>>> # What are the odds?                                     ③
>>> for num in numbers:                                      ④
...     if num % 2 != 0:                                     ⑤
...         odd_numbers.append(num)                          ⑥
...
>>> print "the odd numbers are:", odd_numbers               ⑦
the odd numbers are: [1, 3, 5, 7, 9]
>>>
```

You must have noticed a few things, such as the lack of semicolons as statement separators. Let's work through this code one line at a time to see what else is new and different compared to Java.

1. In the first line, we are declaring a *list* of numbers. Lists are one of the built-in data structures in Python, along with *tuples*, *dicts*, and *sets*. Notice that we didn't declare any types nor did we use any new keyword to allocate the list.

2. Next, we declare another list, named odd_numbers, which is initialized empty.

3. Moving further down, we find a *comment* starting with the # token. Comments extend to the end of line, just like they do in Java with the // token.

4. Here, we come upon a for loop, which should remind you of a more *English* version of Java's *foreach* loop. Block scopes, like in this for loop or the if conditional in the next line, are denoted using indentation instead of curly ({..}) braces. Using just whitespace indentation to define blocks may sound weird and even prone to errors! But just give it a chance and you'll find it to quickly become second nature. Note that the Python REPL uses ellipsis (...) to indicate a block scope, you don't type the ellipsis. The next three lines start with an ellipsis, which is the scope of this for loop.

5. On this line is an if statement that is quite similar to Java, except for the lack of parentheses. Parentheses around for and if conditional expressions are optional. Include them only when they add clarity. Apart from the for and if constructs shown here, Python also has elif, while, and so forth.

6. Here, we append the current loop number to the odd_numbers list. The list, like almost everything in Python, is an object that supports several operations on it, including the append operation.

7. Finally, we print the results to console. No more typing of the decidedly more verbose System.out. println!

Caution   *Never mix tabs and whitespaces in Python source code.*
While you can use either tabs or whitespace to denote indentation,
mixing the two in the same source file may lead to parsing errors.
My recommendation: just don't use tabs and stick to spaces. Set your
text editor to insert four space characters per tab.

Basic Types

Some of the basic data types in Python are *numbers*, *strings*, and
collections.

Numbers

Numbers come in the following variety.

Type	Example value
int	1000
long	1000L
float	1000.12
complex	1000 + 12j

Although int and long are different data types, in practice, you only
need to worry about them when declaring literal values; that is, literal
longs need to be declared with a L suffix. During arithmetic operations,
Python automatically converts int values to long values as needed. This
also prevents overflow-related bugs.

Note   In Python 3, there's no distinction between int and long;
there's only one arbitrary length integer type.

Strings

As in Java, strings are immutable in Python. String values can be wrapped in either single or double quotes. To differentiate between vanilla ASCII strings and Unicode strings, Python uses the u prefix to denote the latter. Unicode strings provide additional operations related to encoding/decoding from various character sets.

Type	Example value
str	'apple'
unicode	u'äþþĺė'
str	r'C:\temp'

A third type of string is the *raw string* denoted by the r prefix. This is just an indication to the Python parser to not apply any backslash escaping rules to the string. Here's a quick example that illustrates the difference.

```
>>> print 'c:\temp\dir'        ①
c:      emp\dir
>>> print 'c:\\temp\dir'       ②
c:\temp\dir
>>> print r'c:\temp\dir'       ③
c:\temp\dir
>>>
```

1. The \t is interpreted as the *tab* character, resulting in a tab being printed.

2. Escaping the \t with an additional backslash helps, but makes the string harder to read.

3. Now the \t is left as-is since the r prefix is used to mark the string as a *raw* string.

17

As you can imagine, raw strings are extremely useful when denoting file system paths or regular expressions.

Note   In Python 3, all strings are `unicode` by default. Strings without encoding are treated as bytes without any text semantics.

Collections

The built-in Python collections come in four varieties.

Collection Type	Java Equivalent	Example Value
list	java.util.ArrayList	['apple', 'ball', 'ball']
tuple	java.util.ArrayList	('apple', 'ball', 'ball')
dict	java.util.HashMap	{'fruit': 'apple', 'toy': 'ball'}
set	java.util.HashSet	{'apple', 'ball'}

Each of these collection types provides several useful operations, such as sort, subsequence, and so forth. Another key property is that all these data types are heterogeneous and can host values of differing data types. Think Collection<Object> and not Collection<T>.

Tip   While `tuple` and `list` may look similar, the distinction is that a `tuple` is immutable.

Having these basic collections built into the language syntax is immensely useful. It makes a lot of day-to-day code quite succinct without the overhead of importing collection APIs and their associated baggage.

Fun with Lists

Lists are the workhorse data structure in Python and I exaggerate only slightly when I say that mastering them is the key to mastering Python! Although earlier I said that they are like java.util.ArrayList, they are truly much more than that. But first, let's look at a short example demonstrating their use as a basic array.

```
>>> numbers = [0, 1, 2, 'three', 4, 5, 6, 7, 8, 9]     ①
>>> numbers[0]                                          ②
0
>>> numbers[-1]                                         ③
9
```

1. The first thing to note is that the numbers list is not homogeneous and can host values of different types, be it numbers, strings, other objects or even other lists!

2. The individual element access is using the well-known array index syntax: L[index].

3. Python allows passing in a negative value for the index, in which case, it adds the length of the list to the index and returns the corresponding element.

Apart from single element access, what sets apart Python lists is the ability to extract element ranges from lists. This is accomplished using the *slice syntax*. Here's how.

```
>>> numbers[0:4]            ①
[0, 1, 2, 'three']

>>> numbers[:4]             ②
[0, 1, 2, 'three']
```

```
>>> numbers[4:]                    ③
[4, 5, 6, 7, 8, 9]

>>> numbers[2:-2]                  ④
[2, 'three', 4, 5, 6, 7]

>>> numbers[0:9:2]                 ⑤
[0, 2, 4, 6, 8]

>>> numbers[::2]                   ⑥
[0, 2, 4, 6, 8]

>>> numbers[::-1]                  ⑦
[9, 8, 7, 6, 5, 4, 'three', 2, 1, 0]
```

1. The slice syntax—L[start:stop]—returns a subsequence of the list as a new list.

2. The start index is optional and when omitted, defaults to 0.

3. The stop index is also optional and defaults to the length of the list.

4. A negative stop index counts off from the end, in accordance with the rule described for line 3 of this code example.

5. The full slice syntax is actually L[start:stop:step] where the step, when omitted, defaults to 1. Here, we set it to 2 and it skips every other element of the list.

6. Another example showing default values for start and stop.

7. A negative step reverses the direction of iteration.

The copy returned by the slice notation is a shallow copy. I can demonstrate this in the following example:

```
>>> copy = numbers[:]          ①
>>> copy == numbers            ②
True
>>> copy is numbers            ③
False
>>> id(copy), id(numbers)      ④
(3065471404L, 3075271788L)
```

1. Creates a shallow copy

2. The two lists are logically equal. This is similar to comparison using equals() in Java.

3. But the two lists are not the same object. This is similar to comparison using == in Java.

4. We can confirm by checking the object references using the id() built-in function. This is similar to the default hashCode() in Java.

Now let's turn our eyes toward performing operations on lists. The first thing one would want to do with a list is to iterate over its elements. There are a few different variants of list iteration in Python, either using the vanilla *foreach* style syntax or augmenting it with the enumerate, range, and len built-in functions.

```
>>> numbers = [10, 20, 30]
>>> for number in numbers:
...     print number
...
10
20
30
```

21

```
>>> for index, number in enumerate(numbers):
...     print index, number
...
0 10
1 20
2 30

>>> for  index in range(len(numbers)):
...     print index
...
0
1
2
```

Next, let's look at how to mutate lists.

```
>>> toys = ['bat', 'ball', 'truck']
>>> if 'bat' in toys:
...     print 'Found bat!'
...
Found bat!

>>> toys.append('doll')
>>> print toys
['bat', 'ball', 'truck', 'doll']

>>> toys.remove('ball')
>>> print toys
['bat', 'truck', 'doll']

>>> toys.sort()
>>> print toys
['bat', 'doll', 'truck']
```

Lists can also be used as simple stacks and queues.

```
>>> stack = []
>>> stack.append("event")    # Push
>>> event = stack.pop()      # Pop
>>>
>>> queue = []
>>> queue.append("event")    # Push
>>> event = queue.pop(0)     # Pop from beginning
```

There are many more operations that a list provides, such as extend, insert, and reverse. But let's now look at one of the most interesting features of lists: *comprehensions*.

Consider the following code, which computes the factorial of the first few integers:

```
>>> import math

>>> numbers = range(5)
>>> numbers
[0, 1, 2, 3, 4]
>>> factorials = []

>>> for num in numbers:
...     factorials.append(math.factorial(num))
...
>>> factorials
[1, 1, 2, 6, 24]
```

The preceding procedural loop can be replaced by a *functional* one-liner using the built-in map function, as follows:

```
>>> factorials = map(math.factorial, range(5))
```

Python defines list comprehensions using the syntax: `new_list =
[function(item) for item in L]`. We can rewrite the factorial loop using
this syntax, as follows:

```
>>> factorials = [math.factorial(num) for num in range(5)]
```

Tip   List comprehensions are one of the most Pythonic language
features. Anytime that you see or think of a `map(fn, iter)`, it can
be better expressed as `[fn(x) for x in iter]`.

Here's another variant that introduces a conditional in the
comprehension:

```
>>> factorials_of_odds = [math.factorial(num) for num in
range(10) if num % 2 != 0]
```

If the list/object being iterated over is large (or even unbounded), then
a variant of the list comprehension syntax called *generator expressions* can
be used. In the following snippet, `factorials_of_odds` is lazily computed
as you iterate over it.

```
>>> factorials_of_odds = (math.factorial(num) for num in
xrange(10**10) if num % 2 != 0)
```

Syntactically, the only difference between list comprehensions and
generator expressions is that while the former are enclosed in square
brackets, the latter are enclosed in round brackets.

ASIDE

In the *generator expressions* example, I used a function xrange(10**10).
The ** is the exponent operator; that is, 10**10 is 10000000000. The
usual range function, when called with 10**10 as an argument, would
have to allocate and keep in memory a ten billion–elements list. Instead of
preallocating such a big list, xrange returns an iterator, which only when
iterated over, produces elements up to ten billion, one at a time.

With that rather verbose introduction to *lists*, let's turn our attention
toward one of the core building blocks of procedural programming:
functions.

Functions

Functions in Python are quite a bit more flexible than in Java.

- They are first-class objects that can live by themselves
  without the need to be wrapped inside classes. They
  can be created at runtime, assigned to variables, passed
  as arguments to other functions, and returned as values
  from other functions.

- In addition to a simple list of positional parameters,
  Python functions also support named parameters,
  varargs, and keyword-based varargs.

- Python also supports anonymous functions in the form
  of *lambda expressions,* a feature added to Java in 2014
  as part of the Java SE 8 release.

Here's what a function definition in Python looks like:

```
def a_function(arg1, arg2="default", *args, **kwargs):
    """This is a short piece of documentation for this function.
      It can span multiple lines.
    """
    print "arg1:", arg1      # arg1 is a mandatory parameter
    print "arg2:", arg2      # arg2 is an optional parameter
    with a default value
    print "args:", args      # args is a tuple of positional
    parameters
    print "kwargs:", kwargs # kwargs is a dictionary of keyword
    parameters
```

Function definitions begin with the def keyword (Hello, Scala and Groovy!) followed by the parameter list in parentheses. Once again, there are no curly braces, and only the indentation defines the scope of the function body.

Note   For now, please ignore the strange looking asterisk prefix in front of `args` and `kwargs` in this function's parameter declaration. It is a special bit of syntax that I'll describe in the next section.

The documentation within triple quotes is called a *docstring*, similar to Javadoc. Calling `help(a_function)` displays this docstring.

```
>>> help(a_function)
Help on function a_function in module __main__:

a_function(arg1, arg2='default', *args, **kwargs)
    This is a short piece of documentation for this function.
    It can span multiple lines.
(END)
```

We don't declare the types of the parameters, relying instead on *duck typing*; that is, as long as the parameter argument has the attributes our function expects to operate upon, we don't care about its real type.

ASIDE

Wikipedia has a nice, concise explanation of duck typing: "A style of typing in which an object's methods and properties determine the valid semantics, rather than its inheritance from a particular class or implementation of an explicit interface." The name of the concept refers to the duck test, attributed to James Whitcomb Riley, which is phrased as follows: "When I see a bird that walks like a duck, and swims like a duck, and quacks like a duck, I call that bird a duck."

In duck typing, a programmer is only concerned with ensuring that objects behave as demanded of them in a given context, rather than ensuring that they are of a specific type. For example, in a non-duck-typed language, you would create a function that requires that the object passed into it be of type Duck to ensure that that function can then use the object's walk and quack methods. In a duck-typed language, the function would take an object of any type, and simply call its walk and quack methods, producing a runtime error if they are not defined.

Let's see how a_function (as defined earlier) behaves when called with different argument values.

```
>>> a_function(10)                              ①
arg1: 10
arg2: default
args: ()
kwargs: {}
```

```
>>> a_function(10, "ten")                                    ②
arg1: 10
arg2: ten
args: ()
kwargs: {}

>>> a_function(10, 20, 30, 40)                               ③
arg1: 10
arg2: 20
args: (30, 40)
kwargs: {}
>>> a_function(10, "twenty", arg3=30, arg4="forty")          ④
arg1: 10
arg2: twenty
args: ()
kwargs: {'arg3': 30, 'arg4': 'forty'}

>>> a_function(arg2="twenty", arg1=10, arg3=30,
arg4="forty")                                                ⑤
arg1: 10
arg2: twenty
args: ()
kwargs: {'arg3': 30, 'arg4': 'forty'}
```

1. Only arg1 is provided; the other parameters are initialized to default values.

2. The positional arguments are provided.

3. This is like Java's varargs. All the positional arguments that aren't explicitly declared in the parameter list are populated in the args tuple.

4. This demonstrates the usage of a keyword or named arguments.

5. The order isn't important when the parameter names are made explicit.

Functions and Tuples

Python functions hold one more trick up their sleeve: support for multiple return values!

```python
def multi_return():
    # These are automatically wrapped up
    # and returned in one tuple
    return 10, 20, 'thirty'

>>> values = multi_return()
>>> print values
(10, 20, 'thirty')
```

When a function returns multiple comma-separated values, Python automatically wraps them up into a tuple data structure and returns that tuple to the caller. This is a feature called *automatic tuple packing*. You may make this packing more explicit by wrapping up your return values in a tuple yourself but this is neither required, nor encouraged.

The really interesting part comes when this feature is combined with its counterpart, *automatic tuple unpacking*. Here's how it works:

```python
>>> numbers = (1, 2, 3)          ①
>>> print numbers
(1, 2, 3)

>>> a, b, c = (1, 2, 3)          ②
>>> print a, b, c
1 2 3
```

```
>>> a, b, c = multi_return()     ③
>>> print a, b, c
10 20 thirty
```

1. Here, numbers is just a regular tuple.

2. The tuple on the right of the assignment got *unpacked* into the variables on the left.

3. The tuple returned from multi_return got *unpacked* into the variables on the left.

What happened here is that first, Python packed the multiple return values from multi_return into a single tuple. Then, it transparently unpacked the returned tuple and assigned the contained values to the corresponding variables on the left of the assignment.

For this to work, the number of variables on the left must match the number of elements being returned by the called function; otherwise, an error is raised.

```
>>> a, b = multi_return()
ValueError: too many values to unpack
```

Now that you know how tuple packing and unpacking works, let's revisit the strange looking asterisks in *args and **kwargs that we encountered in the previous section. The leading single asterisk is Python notation to *unpack* the tuple values while the leading double asterisk unpacks the dict values. Here's an example that demonstrates this:

```
def ternary(a, b, c):
    print a, b, c

>>> ternary(1, 2, 3)
1 2 3

>>> args = (1, 2, 3)
>>> ternary(args)
```

```
TypeError: ternary() takes exactly 3 arguments (1 given)

>>> ternary(*args)   # Unpacks the args tuple before function call
1 2 3

>>> kwargs = {'a': 1, 'b': 2, 'c': 3}
>>> ternary(kwargs)
TypeError: ternary() takes exactly 3 arguments (1 given)

>>> ternary(**kwargs) # unpacks the dictionary before function
call
1 2 3
```

Functions Inside Functions

Now that you are familiar with the basic function definition syntax, let's look at a more advanced example. Consider the following function:

```
def make_function(parity):                                          ①
    """Returns a function that filters out `odd` or `even`
        numbers depending on the provided `parity`.
    """
    if parity == 'even':
        matches_parity = lambda x: x % 2 == 0                        ②
    elif parity == 'odd':
        matches_parity = lambda x: x % 2 != 0
    else:
        raise AttributeError("Unknown Parity: " + parity)           ③

    def get_by_parity(numbers):                                     ④
        filtered = [num for num in numbers if matches_parity(num)]
        return filtered

    return get_by_parity                                            ⑤
#
```

There's a lot to digest here! Let's take it line by line.

1. Here, we begin defining a function named make_ function, starting with the docstring.

2. Next, we use the lambda keyword to define a one line, anonymous function that we assign to matches_parity. The lambda function assigned to matches_parity depends on the value of the parity function argument.

3. If the parameter argument value is neither odd nor even, we raise the built-in AttributeError exception.

4. We now define a get_by_parity function within the enclosing function's body. You'll notice that the value of matches_parity is used here. This is a *closure*. It is similar to capturing final fields from enclosing scopes inside anonymous class declarations in Java. In fact, the lambda functionality in Java 8 is much closer to this Python feature than Java anonymous classes.

5. Finally, we return the get_by_parity function object from make_function.

Functions in Python are first-class objects of type function. They can be passed around and assigned to variables, just like any other object. In this case, when someone calls make_function, it returns another function whose definition depends on the parameter passed to make_function. Let's see how this works with a quick example.

```
>>> get_odds = make_function('odd')            ①
>>> print get_odds(range(10))                  ②
[1, 3, 5, 7, 9]
```

```
>>> get_evens = make_function('even')          ③
>>> print get_evens(range(10))
[0, 2, 4, 6, 8]
```

1. We called make_function with odd as the parity parameter value, and it returns to us a function that we assign to the get_odds variable.

2. Now, for all practical purposes, get_odds is just another function. We invoke it by passing in a list of numbers (range(10) returns a list of 0..10) and out comes a filtered list of odd numbers.

3. We can repeat this exercise for the even parity and verify that make_function is working as expected.

Tip   "Functions as first-class objects" is a powerful idea to digest and necessitates a change in how you structure your programs. Coming from a Java background to Python, you must learn to resist the urge to model everything as a class. After all, not everything is a noun and some things are best described using verbs![1]

A lot can be accomplished using functions and Python's built-in data structures like lists and dicts. In doing so, you'll find that more often than not, your programs turn out to be simpler and easier to understand.

---

[1]See steve-yegge.blogspot.com/2006/03/execution-in-kingdom-of-nouns.html

Classes

Everything in Python is an object and as you'd expect, the way to create objects is to start from classes. Consider the following definition of a simple Person class.

```python
class Person(object):
    def __init__(self, first, last):
        self.first = first
        self.last = last

    def full_name(self):
        return "%s %s" % (self.first, self.last)

    def __str__(self):
        return "Person: " + self.full_name()
```

As in Java, object is at the root of the class hierarchy but unlike Java, it needs to be specified explicitly in Python (although not in Python 3).[2] Inheritance declarations do not use a special keyword like extends. Instead, the parent class' name is enclosed within parentheses after the declaring class's name.

The __init__ method is the *initializer* method and is analogous to the Java class constructor. There is also a *constructor* method called __new__ but you won't use it unless you are doing metaprogramming like writing factory classes, and so forth. Within __init__, all the instance fields – called *attributes* in Python – are initialized. Note that we did not have to pre-declare all the attributes of the class.

---

[2]You may skip specifying object as the base class in Python 2, but it'll have implications as explained in New-style Classes - https://www.python.org/doc/newstyle/

The first argument of all instance methods is self. It is the this reference that is implicit in Java but made explicit in Python. Note that the literal name self isn't mandatory; you could name it whatever you want. If you named it current, then full_name would be defined as:

```
# `current` instead of the conventional `self`
def full_name(current):
    return "%s %s" % (current.first, current.last)
```

ASIDE

I've sneaked in an example of string interpolation in the full_name method definition. Python's string interpolation works on tuple arguments and is similar to Java's String.format(s, arg...). There's another variant that works on named parameters and takes a dictionary argument:

```
>>> "The name is %(last)s, %(first)s %(last)s" % {'first': 'James', 'last': 'Bond'}
'The name is Bond, James Bond'
```

The double underscore notation used in the __init__ method name is a Python convention for declaring *special* methods. The __str__ is another special method. Its behavior is exactly like that of the toString() method in Java. I'll explain what makes these methods special when we talk about protocols.

Now here is some example usage of this Person class.

```
>>> person = Person('Clark', 'Kent')   ①

>>> print person                       ②
Person: Clark Kent

>>> print person.first                 ③
Clark
```

```
>>> print person.full_name()          ④
Clark Kent

>>> print Person.full_name(person)     ⑤
Clark Kent
```

1. Object creation is just as it is in Java, except that you don't need to use the new keyword.

2. `print` is equivalent to `System.out.println()` and it'll call the argument's `__str__` method, just like the latter calls to `toString()`.

3. The fields of the class, called *attributes* in Python, are accessed using the dotted syntax.

4. Methods are accessed using the dotted syntax too. Although `self` is explicit during the method definition, it is implicitly passed when the method is called on an object.

5. But you can make it explicit by calling the method from the class and passing in an instance. Can't do *that* in Java!

You'll notice that we didn't declare whether our fields are private or public. We just accessed them as if they are public. In fact, Python does not have the concept of visibility at all! Everything is just public. If you wish to indicate to the user of your class that a particular attribute or method is an internal implementation detail, then the *convention* is to prefix the attribute/method name with a single underscore and the person using the code will know to tread carefully.

Inheritance

Python supports single inheritance as well as multiple inheritance; that is, the inheritance model is closer to C++ than Java. With multiple inheritance, there's always the question of how methods are resolved when declared at multiple places in the class hierarchy. In Python, the *method resolution order* is in general, depth-first. The class attribute __mro__ can be inspected to check the actual method resolution order being used for the class.

Here's a SuperHero class that extends the Person class that we previously defined. We've added one new attribute, nick, and one new method, nick_name, in the SuperHero class.

```
class SuperHero(Person):
    def __init__(self, first, last, nick):
        super(SuperHero, self).__init__(first, last)
        self.nick = nick

    def nick_name(self):
        return "I am %s" % self.nick
```

super works like it does in Java, but once again, you need to be explicit about the class at which it should start climbing up. Let's see how SuperHero behaves in a few examples.

```
>>> p = SuperHero("Clark", "Kent", "Superman")
```

```
>>> p.nick_name()
I am Superman
```

```
>>> p.full_name()
'Clark Kent'
```

```
>>> type(p)                                    ①
<class '__main__.SuperHero'>
```

```
>>> type(p) is SuperHero
True
```

```
>>> type(type(p))
<type 'type'>

>>> isinstance(p, SuperHero)          ②
True
>>> isinstance(p, Person)
True

>>> issubclass(p.__class__, Person)    ③
True
```

1. The built-in type() function gives the type of any object. The *type* of a class object is type. The __main__ that you see in the class name here is just the default namespace in which Python places your objects. You'll learn more about namespaces in the "Organizing Code" section.

2. The isinstance() built-in function is the Python counterpart of Java's instanceof operator and the Class.isInstance() method.

3. Similarly, the obj.__class__ attribute is like Java's obj.class field.

Polymorphism

Let's look at the canonical example that is used to demonstrate polymorphic behavior, the *shape*.

```
class Square(object):
    def draw(self, canvas):
        ...
```

```
class Circle(object):
    def draw(self, canvas):
        ...
```

Given these two Square and Circle classes, the Java developer inside you would already be thinking of extracting a Shape class or interface that defines the draw(canvas) method. *Resist that urge!* Since Python is dynamic, the following code works just fine without an explicit Shape class:

```
shapes = [Square(), Circle()]
for shape in shapes:
    shape.draw(canvas)
```

There is no real advantage to having a common Shape base class that defines draw(canvas) since there's no static type check to enforce that anyway. If the objects in the shapes list did not implement draw(canvas), you'll find that out at runtime. In short, use inheritance for shared behavior, not for polymorphism.

Getting Dynamic!

So far, what we've seen of classes in Python is pretty tame. There's nothing that you couldn't accomplish in Java. Time to make it interesting! Consider the following:

```
>>> p = SuperHero("Clark", "Kent", "Superman")          ①

>>> def get_last_first(self):                           ②
...     return "%s, %s" % (self.last, self.first)
...
>>> Person.last_first = get_last_first                   ③

>>> print p.last_first()                                 ④
Kent, Clark
```

1. We start with an instance of the SuperHero class.

2. Next, we define a new top-level function named
    get_last_first().

3. Then we assign the reference of the get_last_
    first() function to a new attribute named last_
    first of the Person class.

4. Thanks to the previous step, all instances of the
    Person class, including instances of derived classes,
    have now sprouted a new method.

To summarize, what we've done here is bound a new function as an
instance method to the Person class. Once bound, the method becomes
available to all instances of the Person class, including those already created!

This technique can also be used to define a new implementation for
an existing method. Doing so is usually called *monkey patching* and is
generally frowned upon in the Python community since it can quite easily
cause surprising and unexpected behavior.

Now that we've seen how we can add behavior to a class after the fact,
can we go the other way and *remove* behavior? Sure!

```
>>> print p.last
Kent
>>> del p.last
>>> print p.last
Traceback (most recent call last):
  File "<stdin>", line 1, in <module>
  AttributeError: 'SuperHero' object has no attribute 'last'
```

```
>>> del Person.full_name
>>> p.full_name()
Traceback (most recent call last):
  File "<stdin>", line 1, in <module>
  AttributeError: 'SuperHero' object has no attribute 'full_name'

>>>
```

Because Python is dynamically typed, accessing non-existent fields and methods causes exceptions at runtime. Conversely, we can define new attributes at runtime!

```
class Person(object):
    ...

    def __getattr__(self, item):
        # This special method is called when normal attribute
        lookup fails
        if item is 'hyphenated_name':
            return lambda x: "%s-%s" % (x.first, x.last)
        else raise AttributeError(item)
```

```
>>> p = Person('Clark', 'Kent')
>>> p.hyphenated_name()
'Clark-Kent'
```

Imagine the amount of bytecode rewriting trickery you would have to do to achieve this same effect in Java! Case in point, think of the code gymnastics that Java mock libraries are forced to go through. In Python, mocks are trivial to implement using __getattr__ and __setattr__.

41

Protocols

Protocols are like Java interfaces in that they define one or more methods that offer a particular behavior. However, unlike Java interfaces, protocols are not explicitly defined in source code. The closest equivalent would be the equals(), hashcode(), and toString() methods in Java. These methods aren't part of any explicit interface. Yet, we have an implicit convention[3] that these methods will be invoked in certain situations. So it is with Python protocols.

The Python language defines several different protocols such as sequences, numeric, containers, and so forth. These protocols manifest themselves in terms of special syntactic support in the language grammar. Pretty much every language syntax in Python is implemented in terms of protocols, and thus, can be made to work with your own types by implementing the relevant protocols.

Let me explain this further using one of the protocols, the *Container* protocol, as an example. Consider the following OrderRepository class definition, which provides access to a database backed collection of Order objects.

Caution   Please do not use this example as the basis of production code! It is wide open to SQL Injection attacks. For relational database access, consider using the SQLAlchemy library discussed in Chapter 3.

---

[3]A convention documented in the Java Language Specification, but a convention nevertheless; not a source code level contract.

```python
class OrderRepository(object):
    ...
    def __contains__(self, key):
        return 1 == db.query("select count(1) from Orders where
id='%s'" % key)

    def __getitem__(self, key):
        return Order(db.query("select * from Orders where
id='%s'" % key))

    def __setitem__(self, key, value):
        d = value.as_dict()
        update_params = ", ".join( ["%s = '%s'" % x for x in
d.iteritems()] )
        db.update("update Orders set %s where id='%s'" %
(update_params, key)
```

I've elided the full class definition and only shown the three methods that are part of the Container protocol. Since OrderRepository can now be said to implement the Container protocol, it allows us to use it in the following way:

```python
>>> orders = OrderRepository(db)
>>> if "orderId123" in orders:           ①
...       order = orders["orderId123"]    ②
...       order.status = "shipped"
...       orders["orderId123"] = order    ③
>>>
```

1. Because we've implemented the __contains__ method for the OrderRepository, we can now use the if x in y syntax to operate on it. What's happening under the covers is that Python is translating that if statement into if orders.__contains__("orderId123").

43

2. Similarly, the __getitem__ method unlocks
    the dictionary like access using the order id,
    translating the key lookup to orders.__getitem__
    ("orderId123").

3. Finally, dictionary-like assignment works via the
    __setitem__ method call.

You can think of this as operator overloading or syntactic sugar,
whichever fits your mental model!

Table 2-1 lists of some of the other protocols that Python supports and
the syntax that they power.

Table 2-1. *Protocols in Python*

Protocol	Methods	Supports Syntax
Sequences	Support slice in __getitem__, etc.	seq[1:2]
Iterators	__iter__, next	for x in collection:
Comparison	__eq__, __gt__, __lt__, ...	x == y, x > y, x < y, ...
Numeric	__add__, __sub__, __and__, ...	x + y, x - y, x & y, ...
String like	__str__, __unicode__, __repr__	print x
Attribute access	__getattr__, __setattr__	obj.attr
Context Managers	__enter__, __exit__	with open('out.txt') as f: f.read()

Organizing Code

The most basic unit of source code organization in Python is the *module*, which is just a .py file with Python code in it. This code could be functions, classes, statements or any combination thereof. Several modules can be collected together into a *package*. Python packages are just like Java packages, with one difference: the directory corresponding to a package *must* contain an *initializer* file named __init__.py. This file can be empty or it can optionally contain some bootstrap code that is executed when the package is first imported.

Suppose we have a code base organized, as follows:

```
.
|-- cart.py
|-- db
|   |-- __init__.py
|   |-- mysql.py
|   +-- postgresql.py
+-- model
    |-- __init__.py
    +-- order.py
```

Given this directory listing, we can see that there are two *packages*: db and model. There are four *modules*: cart, mysql, postgresql, and order.

Importing code

Importing code defined in one file (or *module*, in Python terms) into another is accomplished using the import statement. The import statement works pretty much like it does in Java: it brings the declarations from the target module into the current namespace.

There are two syntactical variants of the import statement. The first one is in the familiar Java style, import ... while the second one follows a from ... import ... pattern.

Suppose we have a class named SellOrder defined in the order module; that is, inside the order.py file:

```
$ cat model/order.py
```

```
class SellOrder(object):
    ...
    ...
```

There are a few different ways in which we can *import* and use this class in our main app, cart.py.

```
import model
```

```
sell_order = model.order.SellOrder()
```

In this example, we use the import <package|module> syntax to import the target *package*–model–into the current namespace and then use a dotted notation to get to our SellOrder class. We can use the same syntax to import the specific *module* instead of the containing *package*:

```
import model.order
```

```
sell_order = order.SellOrder()
```

Here, we imported the order *module* directly. Note the distinction between the way the import syntax works in Java and in Python. In Java, we always import a *class* from within our package hierarchy. In Python, an import ... statement can *only* be used to import *packages* or *modules*. If you want to access a class or function definition, you must refer to it via the containing module. Or use the alternate syntax, from <package|module> import <item>:

```
from model.order import SellOrder
```

```
sell_order = SellOrder()
```

Here, we use the from `<package|module>` import `<item>` syntax variant that directly imports SellOrder into the current namespace. This style of import can be used to import any top-level item from within the source module, be it a function, class, or variable definition.

Python offers one more enhancement over Java imports: the ability to rename the import using the **as** keyword.

```
from model.order import TYPES as ORDER_TYPES
from db import TYPES as DATABASE_TYPES

print ORDER_TYPES
# ['buy', 'sell']

print DATABASE_TYPES
# ['mysql', 'postgresql']
```

As you can imagine, this feature comes in very handy when trying to avoid namespace conflicts without having to use the full package/module hierarchy for disambiguation like we do in Java.

Tip   In Java, each `.java` file must contain only class or interface declarations at the top level. Moreover, in typical usage, each such file has just one public class or interface defined. Python modules have no such restrictions. It is perfectly fine to create modules with just functions or just classes or a mix of both. Do not restrict yourself to just one class or function definition per module. This is not only unnecessary, but also considered a bad practice. Instead, strive to collect constructs having conceptual similarity into one module.

The main() Method

Now that we've organized our application's source code into multiple files, you must be wondering, what defines the entry point for the application? As Java programmers, `public static void main` is forever burned into our brains! What's the equivalent in Python?

There is no formal notion of an *application entry point* in Python. Instead, when Python executes a file; for example, when you run `python foo.py`, execution begins at the start of the file and all statements defined at the top-level are executed in order until we reach the end of the file. Consider a file named `odds.py` that contains the following code:

```
# odds.py

def get_odds(numbers):
    odds = [n for n in numbers if n % 2 != 0]
    return odds

odds_until = 10

numbers = range(odds_until)

print get_odds(numbers)
```

When this file is executed by running `python odds.py` from your favorite operating system shell, the Python interpreter starts at the top, runs down the file till it finds the definition of the `get_odds` function. It makes note of this function by adding its name to the current namespace. It does so by making an entry in a lookup table that it maintains for each namespace. Once done with adding `get_odds` to the current namespace's lookup table, Python then skips the rest of the function declaration since statements inside the function's body aren't at the *top level*.

Moving further down the file, Python encounters the declaration of the `odds_until` variable and executes that statement causing the value 10 to be assigned to it. Once again, an entry is made in the current namespace's lookup table for the `odds_until` variable.

On the next line, it encounters an assignment statement that involves a function named range. Python looks up this function in the current namespace, where it can't find it. It then looks for it in the *built-in* namespace and finds it there. Recall that the *built-in* namespace is equivalent to java.lang.*—things defined here don't have to be explicitly imported. Having found the range function, it calls it assigning the return value to numbers. As you can guess by now, another entry is made for numbers in the current namespace.

Proceeding further, we reach the last line of the file where there's a call to get_odds with numbers as a parameter. Since both these names have entries in the current namespace, Python has no trouble calling get_odds with the list of numbers. Only at this point in time is the get_odds function body parsed and executed. The return value is then supplied to print, which writes it out to the console, as follows:

```
$ python odds.py
[1, 3, 5, 7, 9]
$
```

Having seen how Python executes a script, we can try and simulate a *main* method, as follows:

```
# odds.py

def get_odds(numbers):
    odds = [n for n in numbers if n % 2 != 0]
    return odds

def main():
    odds_until = 10
    numbers = range(odds_until)
    print get_odds(numbers)

main()
```

All we've done here is wrapped up all our top-level statements into a function that we conveniently gave the name of main! We call this function at the end of the file, in effect, making main the entry point of our app.

Let's complete our Java-like main method implementation by taking care of the arguments to main; that is, the args in public static void main(String[] args). In Java, all command-line parameters passed to the application during launch would be populated in the args arrays. In Python, this information is available using the built-in sys standard library module. This module defines sys.argv, which is a list of the command-line arguments passed to the Python script on startup. The first value in the list, sys.argv[0] is the name of the script itself. The remaining items in this list are the command-line arguments, if any.

Let's modify our odds.py script to take the number, until which we should print odd numbers as a command-line parameter, which we retrieve using the sys module.

```python
# odds.py

def get_odds(numbers):
    odds = [n for n in numbers if n % 2 != 0]
    return odds

def main(args):
    try:
        odds_until = int(args[1])
    except:
        print "Usage: %s <number>" % sys.argv[0]
        sys.exit(1)

    numbers = range(odds_until)
    print get_odds(numbers)

import sys
main(sys.argv)
```

In this modified odds.py, we invoke the main function with the list of command-line arguments as a parameter. Within main, we initialize the odds_until variable using the first command-line argument. If this fails for any reason, we print a helpful message on how to use the script before exiting with a 1 error code. Here's how this modified example works in practice:

```
$ python odds.py
Usage: odds.py <number>
$ python odds.py abc
Usage: odds.py <number>
$ python odds.py 15
[1, 3, 5, 7, 9, 11, 13]
$
```

Finally, we have a main function that works like Java! It even looks like the main method in Java; def main(args) is more or less identical to public static void main(String[] args) once all the type-related declarations are dropped.

However, there's a wrinkle here that I wish to talk about. Imagine that we found our get_odds function to be so useful that we wanted to use it as a utility function elsewhere in our project's codebase. Since we just talked about modules, the obvious way would be to just use odds.py as a module and import the module wherever we find the use of this utility function. For example, in demo.py:

```
# demo.py

import odds

print odds.get_odds(range(10))
```

When we run this demo.py script, we expect it to import the odds module and then use the get_odds defined in there to print the odd numbers till ten. Instead, here's what happens:

```
$ python demo.py
Usage: demo.py <number>
$
```

That's odd. Why are we getting this message? We passed in 10 as an argument to get_odds in demo.py. Which other <number> is it expecting? In fact, even though the message says "Usage: **demo.py**", this usage message looks very much like the one we defined inside odds.py.

Here's what is actually happening. When Python imports a *module*, it actually *executes* that module, just as it would have if the module were run as a script! During the execution of demo.py, when Python encounters the import odds statement, it first attempts to locate the odds.py file. Having found it, Python executes the entire file, just as I described in our discussion earlier. Specifically, it executes the following piece of top-level code in odds.py:

```
import sys
main(sys.argv)
```

Since there was no command-line parameter supplied during execution of demo.py, the value of sys.argv[1] is missing. This raises an exception within main(), which causes the *Usage* message to get printed. Moreover, since the actual command executed in this case was python demo.py, the value of sys.argv[0] is demo.py and not odds.py. This explains the output message.

To use odds as a module, we would have to remove all top-level statements from it. In fact, this is a very important point!

Caution   Unless you have a very good reason, *do not define any side effect–causing top-level statements in your modules.* If you do so, these statements will be executed whenever your module is imported causing all sorts of headaches.

Here's a modified odds.py, stripped of all top-level code:

```
# odds.py

def get_odds(numbers):
    odds = [n for n in numbers if n % 2 != 0]
    return odds
```

Now, running the demo.py script yields the expected output.

```
$ python demo.py
[1, 3, 5, 7, 9]
```

Having made this change, while we gained the ability to use odds as a module, we lost the ability to run it as a script. Wouldn't it be nice if we could do both? Even in Java land, just because a class defines a main method does not mean that it can't be imported and used as a vanilla class elsewhere!

To achieve this module/script duality, we'll have to dig a little bit deeper into the notion of *namespaces.*

I've mentioned the term *namespace* several times in this chapter without defining it in more detail. In computer science terms, we understand namespaces as isolated contexts or containers for names. Namespaces allow us to group logical things together and allow reuse of names without causing conflicts.

During program execution, whenever a module is imported, Python creates a new namespace for it. The name of the module is used as the name of the namespace. Thus, all that a piece of code such as odds. get_odds(...) is doing is invoking the get_odds function in the odds namespace. When a namespace qualifier is left out, then the object is looked up in the current namespace or failing that, in the built-in namespace.

At runtime, you can get access to the namespace encapsulating your code by referring to the special __name__ variable. This variable is always bound to the current namespace. Let's see an example of __name__ in action by modifying our demo.py and odds.py scripts.

```
# odds.py

print "In odds, __name__ is", __name__

def get_odds(numbers):
    odds = [n for n in numbers if n % 2 != 0]
    return odds
```

```
# demo.py

import odds

print "In demo, __name__ is", __name__

print odds.get_odds(range(10))
```

Now when we run the demo script, we see this output:

```
$ python demo.py
In odds, __name__ is odds
In demo, __name__ is __main__
[1, 3, 5, 7, 9]
```

As we just discussed, on import, the odds module is bound to a namespace with the same name; that is, odds. Hence, in the context of code within odds.py, the value of the __name__ variable is odds. However, for code in demo.py, we see that the value of __name__ is the curiously named __main__. This is a special namespace that Python assigns to the *main* context of your application. In other words, the entry point of your application (typically, the script that is executed by Python) is assigned the namespace __main__.

We can put this knowledge to use to achieve the script/module duality.

Here is our odds.py file once again, in a form that can be executed directly as a Python script, but can't be imported as a module.

```python
# odds.py

def get_odds(numbers):
    odds = [n for n in numbers if n % 2 != 0]
    return odds

def main(args):
    try:
        odds_until = int(args[1])
    except:
        print "Usage: %s <number>" % sys.argv[0]
        sys.exit(1)

    numbers = range(odds_until)
    print get_odds(numbers)
import sys
main(sys.argv)
```

We will wrap up the top-level code behind a check for the current namespace:

```
# odds.py

def get_odds(numbers):
    odds = [n for n in numbers if n % 2 != 0]
    return odds

def main(args):
    try:
        odds_until = int(args[1])
    except:
        print "Usage: %s <number>" % sys.argv[0]
        sys.exit(1)

    numbers = range(odds_until)
    print get_odds(numbers)

if __name__ == '__main__':
    import sys
    main(sys.argv)
```

As you can see, we took the side-effect causing top-level code, namely the invocation of the main() function, and put it behind a conditional that checks if the current namespace is __main__. When odds.py is run as a script; that is, it is the entry point of the application, the value of __name__ will be __main__. Thus, we will enter the conditional block and run that piece of code. On the other hand, when odds.py is imported as a module, the value of __name__ will be odds and not __main__. Thus, the block of code behind the conditional is skipped.

As you read more and more Python code, you'll come across the `if __name__ == '__main__'` construct all the time. It is a standard idiom used in Python programs to get the effect of a *main* method. Python's creator, Guido van Rossum, has written a nice blog post on writing idiomatic Python `main()` functions[4] that takes this idea even further.

Summary

We covered quite a bit of ground in this chapter. We started with a look at the basic syntax and built-in types that Python provides. We then moved on to the building blocks of functions and classes. We then familiarized ourselves with Python's implicit interfaces; that is, protocols. Finally, we learned about organizing source code into modules and packages.

While this book ends our discussion of Python language syntax over here, there's more to Python than this! Some of the advanced topics that we didn't discuss include *decorators, properties, generators, context managers,* and *I/O*. These are topics you'll find yourself exploring once you get comfortable writing basic Python code. To help you along in your learning, I've compiled some useful resources in "References" section at the end of this book.

---

[4]See `http://www.artima.com/weblogs/viewpost.jsp?thread=4829`

CHAPTER 3

The Ecosystem

As software developers, we know that when evaluating a programming language, we need to look at not just the core language itself, but also at the ecosystem of libraries and tools for the language. The richness of this ecosystem often determines how productive you'd be when writing software in the language.

In this chapter, I describe the Python ecosystem and share some of the more popular tools and frameworks to get you started with Python development.

A Rich Ecosystem

In the Java world, we know that Java is much more than the language itself. There's the JVM, the Java language runtime that allows deploying applications on a variety of hardware and operating system targets. There are the Java SE and EE Standard Libraries, which provide a lot of useful functionality out of the box. And of course, there's an immensely rich variety of third-party libraries and frameworks to choose from. It is the strength of this ecosystem that makes Java a great platform to build upon.

So it is with Python!

Python too can be deployed on different hardware targets like x86, ARM, and MIPS; on multiple operating systems like Linux, Mac OS X,

© Deepak Sarda 2017
D. Sarda, *Python for the Busy Java Developer*, https://doi.org/10.1007/978-1-4842-3234-7_3

Windows, and Solaris. It can even be deployed on other software runtimes like the .NET CLR (IronPython[1]) or the Java virtual machine (Jython[2]).

Python has a great standard library with lots of functionality delivered out of the box. "Batteries included" is often used to describe the richness of the standard library.

Beyond the standard library, the third-party libraries and frameworks landscape is similarly rich, ranging from numerical and scientific computing packages, to NLP, to networking, GUI, and web frameworks. You'd be hard pressed to find a domain for which there isn't already a Python library out there.

To help you get started, I've put together a couple of lists in Tables 3-1 and 3-2 that'll help you pick out the Python counterparts of the Java tools and libraries that you are already familiar with. These lists are by no means exhaustive but I do believe that they represent the most popular options in use today.

Popular Tools

In the Python world, third-party library installation is typically done using a tool named `pip`. It can read the requisite third-party package dependencies for your project from a standardized `requirements.txt` file, and then install/upgrade packages as necessary. If needed, it can even download packages from a central repository named PyPI, short for the Python Package Index. This is the Python world's equivalent of Maven's Central Repository.

---

[1] http://ironpython.net/
[2] http://www.jython.org/

Table 3-1. *Popular Build and Execution Tools*

Java	Python
build.xml/pom.xml	requirements.txt
Maven	pip
Maven Central repository	PyPI
Classpath	PYTHONPATH
HotSpot	CPython

With third-party packages comes the question of how they are located at runtime. Java's solution is the *classpath* and Python's equivalent is the PYTHONPATH. Conceptually, they are similar in that both specify a list of locations where the language runtime should search for packages being imported. Implementation wise, they differ a bit. PYTHONPATH is set as an environment variable; for example, PYTHONPATH=/path/to/foo:/path/to/bar, a syntax similar to the typical system shell's PATH variable. Another flexibility that Python provides is that this library search path can be modified at runtime just by manipulating the sys.path attribute exposed by the built-in system module. As you might have guessed, sys.path is initialized from the value set for the PYTHONPATH environment variable.

I mentioned earlier that there are multiple runtime implementations of the Python language. The canonical implementation is *CPython*, named so because the core of the language runtime is implemented in C. It is the most widely used implementation and regarded as the reference for the Python language. Alternative implementations include Jython, which is Python running on the JVM; IronPython, which is Python running on the .NET Common Language Runtime; and PyPy, which is an upcoming implementation of Python that provides a number of improvements like a runtime JIT compiler, secure sandboxing, and green threads based concurrency.

As a Java developer, you may wish to explore Jython a bit more. Since it is essentially Python code translated to Java bytecode and running inside a Java virtual machine, it allows for easy interop between Python and Java. As an example, you could write high-level business rules in Python and call into a Java rule engine to execute those rules.

Popular Frameworks

Since Python is a dynamic language, there's a class of programming errors that are revealed at runtime, instead of being caught at compile time like they would in a statically typed language. Thus, writing automated tests for your Python programs is even more important than it is in Java. The Python standard library ships with a unit-testing framework creatively named *unittest*, which should serve as good start. If you find that unittest is missing some features you'd like or is just a bit too cumbersome to use, then *pytest* is a good third-party alternative.

Table 3-2. *Popular Development and Testing Frameworks*

Java	Python
JUnit	unittest/pytest
Mockito	unittest.mock
Findbugs/Checkstyle	pylint
Javadoc	Sphinx
Swing	PyQT/PyGTK
Spring Boot	Django/Flask
Hibernate	SQLAlchemy
Velocity/Thymeleaf	Jinja2
Servlets	WSGI
Tomcat/Jetty	Apache/uWSGI

Another tool in the modern developer's arsenal for keeping code quality high is automated static analysis of source code. The findbugs and checkstyle equivalent for Python is pylint. It can enforce a uniform code formatting style, detect basic programming errors, and duplicate blocks of code. And as you would expect, you can integrate it in your IDE as well as CI build server.

If you are building a desktop GUI, then the PyQT and PyGTK libraries are popular options. These are Python wrappers around the popular Qt and GTK libraries, respectively. Both these frameworks are cross-platform, just like Java Swing.

While desktop GUI applications still have their place, it isn't a stretch to say that a majority of new applications being built today are web applications. Python is very well suited to this task. In fact, you may be surprised to know that many of the Internet's most popular websites, like YouTube and Reddit, are written in Python.

Spring Boot is a popular choice for *full stack* web development in the Java world. By *full stack*, I mean a framework that handles everything from frontend user authentication to backend database connectivity and everything in between. The most popular full-stack web development framework for Python is Django. If you are just dipping your toes into web development with Python, I strongly recommend that you start with Django. You'll find it to be a very easy to learn and productive web development environment.

On the other hand, if you are the type of developer who finds full stack frameworks too restrictive to use, then you can mix and match best of breed libraries and roll your own stack. On the database access front, SQLAlchemy is the preeminent option. It provides a low-level DB interface like JDBC, a mid-level Spring JDBCTemplate like interface that provides convenient plumbing around writing raw SQL queries, and finally, a high-level ORM layer like Hibernate. Depending on your requirements, you can choose just the level of abstraction that you need.

Another aspect of web development is generating responses for HTTP requests, typically HTML pages, using a template engine. This is the kind of work for which you'd reach for the Velocity or Thymeleaf libraries over in Java land. Jinja2 is the go-to templating library for Python applications. It has a pleasant syntax, lots of features, and is fairly fast too.

Python web sites are generally deployed using either the Apache web server or a smaller Python specific web server like uWSGI. These web servers rely on a Python web development standard called the Web Server Gateway Interface (WSGI). Think of it as the equivalent of Java servlets in the Python world.

Summary

Due to its long history and popularity, Python has gained a rich ecosystem of libraries, tools, and frameworks that aid software development. We discussed a few of the popular ones in this chapter that should help you get started on your first Python project.

CHAPTER 4

The Zen of Python

We are finally at the end of this short book and I hope that, as promised at the start, you've gained sufficient familiarity with the Python language and ecosystem to start hacking on some Python code of your own.

While you dive in to writing Python code, I urge you to also take some time to read existing Python code written by long time Python programmers. Reading code written by experienced Pythonistas will give you an appreciation for what is considered to be good and idiomatic Python code. Because in the end, it is not just the pure mechanics of the language, but this pervasive appreciation by the community for simple, readable code that makes Python such a joy to use.

And there's no better distillation of this Pythonic mind-set than Tim Peter's "TheZen of Python."[1]

```
antrix@cellar:~$ python
>>> import this

The Zen of Python, by Tim Peters

Beautiful is better than ugly.
Explicit is better than implicit.
Simple is better than complex.
Complex is better than complicated.
```

---

[1]See http://www.wefearchange.org/2010/06/import-this-and-zen-of-python.html

© Deepak Sarda 2017

D. Sarda, *Python for the Busy Java Developer*, https://doi.org/10.1007/978-1-4842-3234-7_4

Flat is better than nested.
Sparse is better than dense.
Readability counts.
Special cases aren't special enough to break the rules.
Although practicality beats purity.
Errors should never pass silently.
Unless explicitly silenced.
In the face of ambiguity, refuse the temptation to guess.
There should be one -- and preferably only one -- obvious way
to do it.
Although that way may not be obvious at first unless you're Dutch.
Now is better than never.
Although never is often better than *right* now.
If the implementation is hard to explain, it's a bad idea.
If the implementation is easy to explain, it may be a good idea.
Namespaces are one honking great idea -- let's do more of those!
>>>

APPENDIX

References

- Code Like a Pythonista: Idiomatic Python

  `http://python.net/~goodger/projects/`
  `pycon/2007/idiomatic/handout.html`

- Generator Tricks for Systems Programmers

  `http://www.dabeaz.com/generators-uk/`

- Java is not Python, either...

  `http://dirtsimple.org/2004/12/java-is-not-`
  `python-either.html`

- Python Ecosystem: An Introduction

  `http://mirnazim.org/writings/python-`
  `ecosystem-introduction/`

- Python Is Not Java

  `http://dirtsimple.org/2004/12/python-is-not-`
  `java.html`

- Secrets of the Framework Creators

  `http://farmdev.com/src/secrets/`

© Deepak Sarda 2017
D. Sarda, *Python for the Busy Java Developer*, https://doi.org/10.1007/978-1-4842-3234-7_5

- Style Guide for Python Code

  http://legacy.python.org/dev/peps/pep-0008/

- The Hitchhiker's Guide to Python!

  http://docs.python-guide.org/en/latest/

Index

A, B, C, D

Command-line arguments, 51

E, F, G, H

Ecosystem
  build and execution tools, 61
  Django, 64
  frameworks, 62, 64
  frameworks landscape, 60
  hardware targets, 59
  Java SE and EE Standard
    Libraries, 59
  Jython, 61
  PyQT and PyGTK libraries, 63
  PYTHONPATH, 61
  SQLAlchemy, 64
  third-party libraries, 60
  third-party libraries and
    frameworks, 59

I

Inheritance, 37–38
IronPython, 60

J, K, L

Java virtual machine (Jython), 60
Jython, 61

M, N, O

Method resolution order, 37

P, Q

Polymorphism, 38–39
Python
  functional programming, 2
  history, 3, 5
  installation, 5
  JVM garbage collectors, 3
  memory management, 3
  object oriented programming, 2
  obj variable, 2
  Python Software Foundation
    License Agreement, 1
  scripts and command-line
    tools, 1
  tools
    built-in functions, 8

© Deepak Sarda 2017

D. Sarda, *Python for the Busy Java Developer*, https://doi.org/10.1007/978-1-4842-3234-7

Python (*cont.*)
    dir function, 9
    dir() function, 10–11
    dir function, 9
    interactive mode, 7
    Java, 6
    .pyc files, 6
    traditional development
      process, 12
  types, 1
  variables and objects, 2
  Zen, 68
Python Enhancement Proposals
    (PEP), 5
Python language features
  attributes, 41
  basic constructs, 14–16
  basic data types
    collections, 18
    numbers, 16
    strings, 17–18
  classes, 34–36
  code organization
    importing code, 45–47
    main() method, 48, 50–54, 56
    module and packages, 45
  dictionaries and sets, 13
  functions, 25–27, 29
  get_last_first() function, 40
  inheritance, 37–38
  inside functions, 31–33
  lists, 19–20, 22, 24–25

  modules and packages, 13
  monkey patching, 40
  object-oriented
    language, 13
  Person class, 40
  polymorphism, 38–39
  protocols, 42, 44
  short code fragments, 13
  SuperHero class, 40
  tuples, 29–30
Python Software Foundation
    License Agreement, 1

R
Read Eval Print Loop (REPL), 7

S
SuperHero class, 37–38

T, U, V
toString() method, 35

W, X, Y
Web Server Gateway
    Interface (WSGI), 64

Z
Zen of Python, 68

Get the eBook for only $5!

Why limit yourself?

With most of our titles available in both PDF and ePUB format, you can access your content wherever and however you wish—on your PC, phone, tablet, or reader.

Since you've purchased this print book, we are happy to offer you the eBook for just $5.

To learn more, go to http://www.apress.com/companion or contact support@apress.com.

Apress®

Printed in the United States
By Bookmasters